Our Dessert Recipes

Copyright 2013, Gooseberry Patch

First Printing, June, 2013

Serve ice cream-topped desserts to a party crowd,
the quick & easy way! Scoop ice cream ahead of time
and freeze in paper muffin liners.

Aunt Maggie's Apple Crisp

Makes 9 servings

4 c. apples, peeled, cored and
    diced
3/4 c. plus 1 T. all-purpose flour,
    divided
1/2 c. sugar
1 T. cinnamon
3/4 c. brown sugar, packed

3/4 c. quick-cooking oats,
    uncooked
1/4 t. baking soda
1/4 t. baking powder
1/8 t. salt
1/2 c. butter

In a bowl, mix together apples, one tablespoon flour, sugar and
cinnamon. Transfer to a greased 8"x8" baking pan. Bake, uncovered,
at 450 degrees for 15 minutes. Remove from oven and reduce heat to
350 degrees. Mix together remaining dry ingredients in a separate bowl.
Cut in butter with pastry blender until crumbly. Arrange topping over
apples and bake for an additional 35 minutes. Serve warm.

Head out to a pick-your-own apple orchard for a day of fresh-air fun. The kids will love it, and you'll come home with bushels of the best-tasting apples for cobblers, pies and crisps!

Baked Caramel Apples

Serves 4 to 6

4 apples, peeled, cored and
    quartered
1 T. butter
1 T. all-purpose flour

1 c. brown sugar, packed
1 c. boiling water
1-1/2 c. mini marshmallows
1 t. vanilla extract

Arrange apples in a buttered 2-quart casserole dish; set aside. Melt butter in a saucepan over low heat; blend in flour. Add brown sugar and water; cook until sugar dissolves. Stir in marshmallows until melted; bring to a boil. Pour mixture over apples. Bake, uncovered, at 350 degrees for 25 to 30 minutes, basting occasionally with sauce.

Nothing says farm-fresh flavor like dollops of whipped cream on a warm home-baked dessert. In a chilled bowl, with chilled beaters, beat a cup of whipping cream on high speed until soft peaks form. Stir in 2 teaspoons sugar and 2 teaspoons vanilla extract.

Just Peachy Bread Pudding

Serves 8

1 loaf French bread, cubed
16-oz. can sliced peaches,
    drained
1/2 c. raisins
2 eggs
2 egg whites
3/4 c. sugar

12-oz. can evaporated milk
2 c. milk
1/2 t. cinnamon
1/4 t. nutmeg
1 t. coconut extract
1 T. vanilla extract

Fill a buttered 3-quart casserole dish with bread cubes, peach slices and
raisins; stir gently and set aside. Combine remaining ingredients; blend
well. Pour egg mixture evenly over bread, gently stirring to coat. Bake,
uncovered, at 350 degrees for 30 to 40 minutes, or until a knife inserted
near the center comes out clean.

Bread pudding is a scrumptious (and thrifty!) way to use up day-old bread. Try French bread, raisin bread or even leftover cinnamon buns for an extra-tasty dessert!

Cinnamon Bread Pudding

Serves 8 to 10

6 eggs
2 c. milk
2 c. half-and-half, divided
1 c. sugar
2 t. vanilla extract

1 loaf cinnamon bread, cubed
1/2 c. brown sugar, packed
1/4 c. butter
1/2 c. corn syrup

In a large bowl, whisk eggs; blend in milk, 1-3/4 cups half-and-half, sugar and vanilla until combined. Stir in bread cubes until lightly moistened. Grease a 2-quart rectangular casserole dish and spread mixture evenly in dish. Bake, uncovered, at 325 degrees for 55 to 60 minutes, until center starts to set. In a small saucepan over low heat, cook brown sugar and butter until butter is melted. Carefully add corn syrup and remaining half-and-half. Cook, stirring constantly, over medium-low heat for one to 2 minutes, until sugar dissolves and mixture is smooth. Serve drizzled over warm pudding.

Share your best berry dessert! Fill a plastic zipping bag with
the dry ingredients; seal. Wrap the bag in a square of homespun
fabric and tie closed with raffia. Give with a recipe card and
a pint of fresh berries from the farmers' market.

Blueberry Crumble

Makes 8 servings

5 c. blueberries
9-inch graham cracker crust
3/4 c. brown sugar, packed
3 T. all-purpose flour
1-1/2 t. vanilla extract

1/4 t. lemon zest
8-oz. container sour cream
1/4 c. soft bread crumbs
1 T. sugar
1 T. margarine, melted

Spoon blueberries into crust; set aside. In a bowl, blend together brown sugar, flour, vanilla, lemon zest and sour cream; spread evenly over blueberries. In a separate bowl, mix together bread crumbs, sugar and margarine; sprinkle over sour cream mixture. Bake, uncovered, at 375 degrees for 40 minutes, or until crumble is golden. Serve warm.

Enjoy fresh berries throughout the year...freeze them during berry season! Spread ripe berries in a single layer on a baking sheet and freeze until solid, then store them in plastic freezer bags. Later, you can pour out just the amount you need.

Blackberry Fool

Serves 4 to 6

3 c. blackberries
1/2 c. sugar
1 T. water
1 T. cornstarch
2 t. lemon juice

3-oz. pkg. cream cheese, softened
1/4 c. powdered sugar
1 t. vanilla extract
1 c. whipping cream

In a large saucepan, combine blackberries and sugar. Bring to a boil over medium heat; cook for several minutes, until berries are tender. Remove from heat. Drain, discarding liquid and any seeds. Place berries in a bowl; set aside. In the same saucepan, combine water and cornstarch. Cook and stir over low heat until smooth. Add berries; cook and stir until thickened, about 5 minutes. Remove from heat; stir in lemon juice and spoon mixture into bowl. Let cool to room temperature; cover and refrigerate until chilled. Shortly before serving time, combine cream cheese, powdered sugar and vanilla in a bowl. Beat with an electric mixer on low speed until blended. Slowly add cream; beat until smooth. Spoon berry mixture into small bowls; dollop with cream cheese mixture.

Give your favorite fruit dessert a fresh new look with a lattice top! Slice a pie crust into one-inch strips and crisscross them on top of the filling. Brush crust with water and a sprinkle of sugar, then bake until golden.

Nectarine & Raspberry Crisp

Makes 6 to 8 servings

2 to 3 nectarines, halved,
  pitted and sliced
1/3 c. apricot preserves
1 t. vanilla extract
2 c. raspberries
1/2 c. all-purpose flour
1/3 c. brown sugar, packed

1/2 t. cinnamon
1/4 t. nutmeg
1/3 c. butter
1 c. granola
1/4 c. toasted slivered almonds,
  coarsely chopped
Garnish: vanilla ice cream

In a lightly greased 8"x8" baking pan, stir together nectarines, preserves and vanilla. Gently fold in raspberries; set aside. In a bowl, combine flour, sugar and spices. Cut in butter until mixture resembles coarse crumbs. Add granola and almonds; toss with a fork until mixed. Sprinkle granola mixture over fruit in pan. Bake, uncovered, at 375 degrees for 25 to 30 minutes, until topping is golden. Serve warm or at room temperature, topped with ice cream.

Toast nuts for extra flavor. Place a single layer of walnuts, pecans or almonds in a skillet. Stir or shake skillet over medium-high heat continually for 5 to 7 minutes. The nuts are done when they start to turn golden and smell toasty.

Strawberry-Pecan Crunch

Serves 6 to 8

1 egg
1 c. sugar
1 c. chopped pecans
2 c. strawberries, hulled and
    sliced
1 c. milk

8-oz. container frozen whipped
    topping, thawed
3.9-oz. pkg. instant vanilla
    pudding mix
1 c. sour cream

Line a baking sheet with aluminum foil and spray with non-stick vegetable spray; set aside. In a bowl, blend together egg and sugar; stir in pecans. Pour into the center of prepared baking sheet. Bake at 350 degrees for 15 minutes. Let cool; crumble half of mixture into an ungreased 13"x9" baking pan. Arrange strawberries over pecan mixture; set aside. Combine remaining ingredients; mix well. Spoon over strawberries; top with reserved pecan mixture. Chill before serving.

Sprinkle wheat germ or flax seed into baking recipes
for extra fiber and a nutty taste.

Strawberry-Almond Trifle

Makes 10 servings

1-1/4 c. milk
1-oz. pkg. instant sugar-free
    vanilla pudding mix
1/4 c. orange juice, divided
1/8 t. nutmeg
8-oz. container frozen whipped
    topping, thawed

1 pound cake
3 c. strawberries, hulled, halved
    and divided
1/4 c. sliced almonds, toasted
    and divided

Pour milk into a large bowl. Add dry pudding mix, 2 tablespoons orange juice and nutmeg; whisk together for one minute. Gently fold in whipped topping; set aside. Slice cake horizontally into 4 layers. Sprinkle layers evenly with remaining orange juice; cut into one-inch cubes. Place half the cake cubes in a trifle bowl or large clear glass bowl. Top cubes with 2-1/2 cups strawberries and 2 tablespoons almonds. Spoon half the whipped topping mixture over berries and almonds. Layer remaining cake cubes and whipped topping. Garnish with reserved berries and almonds. Refrigerate until ready to serve.

To easily soften honey that's crystallized, set the jar in a pan of water and heat on the stove over low heat. In no time at all, the honey will be ready to use in any recipe.

Honey-Custard Bread Pudding

Serves 8 to 10

6 eggs
1/2 t. salt
4 c. milk
2/3 c. plus 2 T. honey, divided
2 T. butter, melted

Optional: 1/2 c. raisins
16-oz. loaf Vienna or French
bread, torn into one-inch
pieces

Beat together eggs and salt in a bowl; set aside. Bring milk just to a boil in a saucepan over low heat; let cool slightly. Stir 2/3 cup honey and butter into milk. Slowly stir eggs into milk mixture; add raisins, if using. Set aside. Place bread in a greased 2-1/2 quart casserole dish. Pour egg mixture over bread. Place casserole dish in another larger pan and pour hot water into the pan to come halfway up the side of the dish. Bake, uncovered, at 325 degrees for one hour, or until set. About 15 minutes before serving, drizzle remaining honey over top.

Serve up cobbler parfaits. In mini Mason jars or small glasses,
alternate scoops of fruit cobbler or crisp and layers of ice cream.
Garnish with whipped topping and a sprig of fresh mint.
Fun for picnics and cookouts!

Buttermilk Pear Cobbler

Makes 8 servings

3 lbs. Anjou or Bosc pears,
    peeled, cored and sliced
1/3 c. brown sugar, packed
1 T. all-purpose flour

1 T. lemon juice
1 t. cinnamon
1/4 t. nutmeg
1/4 t. mace

Combine all ingredients in a large bowl; toss gently to coat pears. Spoon pear mixture into an 8"x8" baking pan coated with non-stick vegetable spray. Drop Biscuit Topping by heaping tablespoonfuls onto pear mixture. Bake at 350 degrees for 45 minutes, or until lightly golden and bubbly.

Biscuit Topping:

1 c. all-purpose flour
1 T. baking powder
3 T. buttermilk

2 T. sugar
1/2 c. chilled butter
3/4 c. milk

In a bowl, mix together flour, baking powder, buttermilk and sugar. Cut in butter with a fork until mixture is crumbly; add milk and mix well.

A touch of whimsy...use Mom's old cow-shaped milk pitcher
to top desserts with cream.

Old-Fashioned Shortcake

Makes 8 to 10 servings

4 c. all-purpose flour
1 t. salt
1/4 c. sugar
2 T. plus 2 t. baking powder

6 T. shortening
1-1/2 c. milk
Garnish: butter, strawberries,
    whipped cream

Sift together dry ingredients in a bowl; add shortening and enough milk
to make a soft dough. Spread in a greased 13"x9" baking pan. Bake,
uncovered, at 350 degrees for 20 to 25 minutes, until golden. Cool;
cut into squares. To serve, split open each square; spread bottom halves
lightly with butter. Top with strawberries and whipped cream; add
top halves.

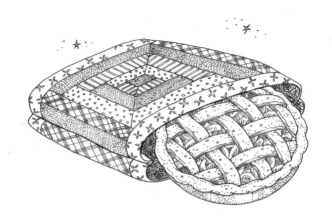

Taking a fresh-baked cobbler or fruit pie to a family
get-together? Keep it warm in a cobbler cozy...simple to make!
Lay two place mats together, wrong-side out. Stitch three sides
together, leaving one of the short ends open. Turn right-side
out...ready to tuck in your dessert!

Buttery Blueberry Cobbler

Serves 8

1/2 c. butter
1 c. all-purpose flour
1-1/4 c. sugar, divided
1 t. baking powder

1/2 c. milk
2 c. blueberries
1 T. lemon juice

Melt butter in an 8"x8" baking pan at 350 degrees; set aside. In a bowl, stir together flour, one cup of sugar and baking powder. Add milk and stir until batter is smooth. Pour evenly over butter; do not stir. Mix berries, lemon juice and remaining sugar in a saucepan over low heat. Bring to a boil and pour evenly over butter and batter; do not stir. Bake, uncovered, at 350 degrees for 45 minutes.

Bake a yummy peach dessert in a pretty vintage enamelware pan...a gift long after the dessert has been enjoyed. Add a tag that says, "To a real peach!" or "I think you're just peachy!"

Wash-Day Peach Pie

Makes 8 servings

1 c. self-rising flour
1 c. sugar
1 c. milk
15-oz. can sliced peaches, drained

1/4 c. butter, sliced
Garnish: vanilla ice cream or
  whipped topping

Stir together flour and sugar in a bowl; add milk and stir until smooth.
Pour batter into a greased 1-1/2 quart casserole dish; spoon peaches over
top. Place butter in center. Bake, uncovered, at 350 degrees for one hour,
or until golden. Serve warm, topped with ice cream or whipped topping.

Tis the sweet, simple things of life which are
the real ones after all.

—Laura Ingalls Wilder

Fresh Peach Pie

Makes 8 servings

1/3 c. all-purpose flour
1 c. plus 1 T. sugar, divided
1/4 c. butter
10 to 12 peaches, peeled, pitted
    and sliced

2 9-inch pie crusts
Optional: ice cream

Combine flour, one cup sugar and butter in a bowl. Mix until crumbly; set aside. Place one pie crust in a 9" pie plate. Arrange a layer of peaches in pie crust; sprinkle one tablespoon of flour mixture on top. Repeat layers with remaining peaches and flour mixture. Add remaining crust; flute edges and cut 4 slits in top crust to vent. Sprinkle with remaining sugar; bake at 350 degrees for 45 minutes, or until crust is golden. Serve warm, topped with a scoop of ice cream, if desired.

For a special dessert in a jiffy, soften 2 pints ice cream and spread in a graham cracker crust, then freeze. Garnish with whipped topping and cookie crumbs or fresh berries. Delicious!

Perfect Arkansas Apple Pie

Serves 8

6 c. Granny Smith apples, peeled,
    cored and thinly sliced
3/4 c. plus 1 t. sugar, divided
1/4 t. salt
1 t. cinnamon
1/8 t. nutmeg

2 T. all-purpose flour
2 T. lemon juice
2 9-inch pie crusts
2 T. butter, diced
1 t. milk

In a large bowl, combine apples, 3/4 cup sugar, salt, cinnamon, nutmeg, flour and lemon juice. Place one pie crust in a 9" pie plate; spoon apple mixture into crust and dot with butter. Top with remaining crust; crimp and seal edges. Make 4 cuts near center to vent. Brush with milk and sprinkle with remaining sugar. Bake at 425 degrees for 45 minutes, until crust is golden.

Set aside a sunny afternoon to host a pie party for friends and neighbors! Set several tables under shady trees and layer them with quilts. Ask friends to bring their favorite pie, and the recipe, to share...you provide the coffee, milk, plates, cups and forks.

Sweet Potato Pie

Makes 8 servings

1/4 c. butter, softened
1/3 c. honey
1/8 t. salt
2 c. sweet potatoes, peeled,
    cooked and mashed
3 eggs, beaten
1/2 c. milk

1 t. vanilla extract
1/2 t. cinnamon
1/2 t. nutmeg
1/2 t. ground ginger
9-inch pie crust
1 c. pecan halves

Blend together butter, honey and salt in a bowl; set aside. In a separate bowl, combine sweet potatoes, eggs, milk, vanilla and spices; stir into butter mixture. Pour into pie crust; top with pecan halves. Bake at 375 degrees for 50 to 55 minutes, until nearly set in center; cool. Store in refrigerator. For the best flavor, cover and chill up to 2 days before serving.

Whole-wheat pastry flour is ideal for adding fiber to
your favorite dessert recipe. Substitute it for some or all of
the all-purpose flour called for. Regular whole-wheat flour
may produce a coarser texture.

Sweet Cherry Triangles

Makes 6 servings

1-1/4 c. all-purpose flour
1 t. sugar, divided
1/4 t. salt
1/2 c. butter, chilled and diced
2 to 3 T. cold water

16-1/2 oz. can dark sweet
  cherries, drained
1/4 c. cherry preserves
3/4 t. cinnamon, divided
2 eggs, beaten

In a bowl, mix together flour, 1/2 teaspoon sugar and salt. Use a pastry blender or 2 knives to cut in butter. Add water, one tablespoon at a time, until a dough begins to form. Wrap and refrigerate for one hour. Roll dough out to a 12-inch by 8-inch rectangle; cut into six 4-inch by 4-inch squares. In a separate bowl, blend cherries, preserves and 1/2 teaspoon cinnamon; spoon equally into the center of each square. Brush egg along the edges of the dough and fold into a triangle. Use the tines of a fork to seal edges. Brush remaining egg over turnovers; sprinkle with remaining sugar and cinnamon. Bake at 425 degrees for 15 minutes, or until golden.

Before adding the top crust to a pie, cut out vents
with a mini cookie cutter...little hearts and stars
leave the prettiest patterns!

Jane's Strawberry-Rhubarb Pie

Serves 8

1/2 c. sugar
1/4 c. quick-cooking tapioca,
    uncooked
1/8 t. salt
2 c. strawberries, hulled and
    halved

2 c. rhubarb, cut into 1-inch
    pieces
Optional: zest of 1 orange
9-inch pie crust
2 T. butter, diced

Combine sugar, tapioca and salt in a large bowl. Add fruit and zest, if using; toss to coat. Spoon into pie crust; dot with butter. Bake at 400 degrees for 20 minutes. Reduce heat to 350 degrees; bake for an additional 20 to 25 minutes.

For a sparkling, golden pie crust, whisk together a little light corn syrup and hot water. Brush the mixture over the unbaked top crust and sprinkle it with coarse sugar before popping into the oven. Beautiful!

Bar Harbor Cranberry Pie

Serves 8

2 c. cranberries
1-1/2 c. sugar, divided
1/2 c. chopped pecans
2 eggs, beaten

1 c. all-purpose flour
1/2 c. margarine, melted
1/4 c. shortening, melted

Lightly butter a 9" glass pie plate; spread cranberries over the bottom.
Sprinkle evenly with 1/2 cup sugar and pecans; set aside. In a separate
bowl, combine eggs and remaining sugar; mix well. Blend in flour,
margarine and shortening; beat well after each addition. Pour over
cranberries; bake at 325 degrees for one hour.

Icy-cold milk is a must with just-baked cookies and pies.
Just for fun, serve it up in vintage half-pint milk bottles.
Don't forget the bendy straws!

Apple & Cheddar Dumplings   *Makes one dozen*

8 9-inch refrigerated pie crusts
1/4 c. shredded Cheddar cheese
12 apples, peeled and cored
1/2 c. mincemeat
1/2 c. butter, divided

3/4 c. sugar, divided
1/4 c. brown sugar, packed
1/4 c. whipping cream
zest of 1/2 lemon

Let pie crusts stand at room temperature for 15 minutes. Cut into twelve 6-inch by 6-inch squares. Spoon one teaspoon Cheddar cheese in the center of each square; top with an apple. Fill the center of each apple with 2 teaspoons mincemeat, one tablespoon butter and one tablespoon sugar. Bring opposite corners of dough together over the apple; pinch together. Blend together brown sugar, cream and lemon zest; brush over dumplings. Arrange dumplings in a buttered 13"x9" baking pan. Bake at 400 degrees for 35 to 45 minutes, until golden. Serve warm with cream.

Whether you call it a rustic pie, a tart or a crostata, it's easy as pie to make! Just lay out a crust on a baking sheet, spoon fruit filling into the center and fold up the crust around the edges. Bake until crust is golden and fruit is bubbly. Yummy!

Rustic Peach Tart

Makes 8 servings

9-inch pie crust
3/4 c. plus 2 T. sugar, divided
1/3 c. all-purpose flour

1/2 t. ground ginger
1/4 t. nutmeg
16-oz. pkg. frozen sliced peaches

On a floured surface, roll out pie crust into a 12-inch circle. Place on an ungreased baking sheet and set aside. Mix 3/4 cup sugar, flour and spices in a large bowl; add frozen peach slices and toss to coat. Spoon peaches onto crust to within 2 inches of edge. Gently fold over edge of crust to form a 2-inch border, pleating as you go. Moisten crust edge with water; sprinkle with remaining sugar. Bake at 425 degrees until golden, about 15 minutes. Reduce temperature to 350 degrees and bake until bubbly, about 30 to 35 minutes more.

For a little extra sweetness, drizzle a powdered sugar glaze
over freshly-baked cakes, pies and cookies. It's easy...
just add 2 tablespoons milk to 1-1/2 cups powdered sugar
and stir until smooth.

Apricot Pockets

Makes one dozen

1/2 c. butter
3-oz. pkg. cream cheese
1 c. all-purpose flour

16-oz. can apricot halves, drained
1 c. sugar
1/2 c. powdered sugar

Mix together butter, cream cheese and flour; form a ball. Wrap in plastic
wrap and refrigerate overnight. Work dough until soft. Roll out on a
floured board. Cut dough into twelve 3-inch by 3-inch squares. Take each
apricot half, roll in sugar and place on a square. Fold up corners to the
center to form a pocket. Place on a parchment paper-lined baking sheet.
Bake at 350 degrees for 20 to 25 minutes, until lightly golden. When
cool, sprinkle with powdered sugar.

An old-fashioned lunchbox is a perfect container to fill with homemade goodies...a great teacher gift too!

Blackberry Turnovers

Makes 6 servings

1-3/4 c. all-purpose flour
1/4 c. plus 1 T. sugar, divided
1/2 t. salt
2/3 c. shortening, chilled
    and diced
2 T. butter, chilled

3 T. water, divided
2 t. cornstarch
16-oz. pkg. frozen blackberries,
    thawed
3/4 t. cinnamon

In a bowl, sift together flour, 1/4 cup sugar and salt; cut in shortening and butter until mixture forms coarse crumbs. Stir in 2 tablespoons water, one tablespoon at a time, until a soft dough forms. Wrap in plastic and refrigerate one hour. Dissolve cornstarch in remaining water; set aside. Combine blackberries, remaining sugar and cinnamon in a saucepan over medium heat, stirring constantly until mixture boils. Stir in cornstarch mixture until filling begins to thicken. Remove from heat and cool. On a lightly floured surface, roll out dough to 1/8-inch thickness and cut out six 6-inch circles. Spoon filling equally into the center of each circle. Fold dough over filling and press edges to seal. Place turnovers on a greased baking sheet. Bake at 400 degrees for 30 minutes, or until golden. Place on a wire rack to cool.

Make dessert a grand finale...serve it
on your prettiest china!

Berry Cream Tarts

Makes one dozen

10-oz. pkg. frozen puff pastry
    shells, thawed
1/4 c. milk
1/4 c. brown sugar, packed
8-oz. pkg. cream cheese, softened

1/2 c. sugar
1/2 t. cinnamon
1-1/2 c. favorite berries
Optional: whipped topping

Place pastry shells on a lightly greased baking sheet. Brush shells with
milk and sprinkle with brown sugar. Bake at 375 degrees for 10 to
15 minutes, until shells turn golden. Remove from oven and remove
tops of shells; set aside. In a bowl, blend together cream cheese, sugar
and cinnamon. Spoon 2 tablespoons of cream cheese mixture into each
shell; top with berries. Replace tops. Return filled shells to oven and bake
an additional 5 minutes, or until filling is warm and bubbly and tops are
golden. Garnish with whipped topping, if desired.

Create a sweet memory and have a tea party for your little girl and her friends. Make it really special: send out pretty invitations, dress up, use real china and treat them to tasty tarts, delicate cakes and herb tea...they'll love it!

Teatime Tassies

Makes 2 dozen

3-oz. pkg. cream cheese, softened
1/2 c. butter, softened
1 c. all-purpose flour
1 egg, beaten

3/4 c. brown sugar, packed
1 t. vanilla extract
3/4 c. finely chopped nuts

Blend together cream cheese and butter in a bowl; stir in flour and mix well. Refrigerate for about 30 minutes. Divide dough into 24 balls; press into greased mini muffin cups. Combine egg, brown sugar, vanilla and nuts; fill cups 3/4 full. Bake at 325 degrees for 25 to 30 minutes, until golden. Let cool 5 minutes before removing tassies from cups.

Dig into Mom's recipe box for that extra-special dessert you remember...and then bake some to share with the whole family.

Nan's Chocolate Pie

Serves 8

1 c. sugar
3 T. cornstarch
1/3 c. baking cocoa
1/4 t. salt
1-1/2 c. milk
3 egg yolks, beaten

1/4 c. butter
1 t. vanilla extract
1/2 t. almond extract
9-inch pie crust, baked
Garnish: whipped cream, grated
    chocolate

In a saucepan over medium-high heat, combine sugar, cornstarch, cocoa and salt. Gradually stir in milk until hot and bubbly. Cook and stir an additional 2 minutes; remove from heat. Stir a small amount of hot mixture into egg yolks. Immediately add yolk mixture to saucepan and cook 2 minutes over low heat, stirring constantly. Remove from heat; add butter and extracts. Stir until smooth. Pour into baked pie crust. Cool in refrigerator; garnish with whipped cream and grated chocolate.

Just-for-me mini desserts are so appealing! Bake cobblers, crisps and pies in individual ramekins...so sweet on a dinner buffet and oh-so easy for guests to serve themselves.

Brown Sugar Puddin' Pies

Makes 15 servings

2.1-oz. pkg. mini phyllo dough
    shells, unbaked
1/2 c. butter, softened
3/4 c. sugar
3/4 c. brown sugar, packed
2 eggs

1/2 c. half-and-half
1/2 t. vanilla extract
1/2 t. nutmeg
Garnish: whipped topping,
    nutmeg

Bake mini shells on a baking sheet at 350 degrees for 4 to 5 minutes;
set aside. In a bowl, blend together butter and sugars until light and
fluffy; blend in eggs, half-and-half and vanilla. Spoon into shells;
sprinkle tops with nutmeg. Bake at 350 degrees for 15 to 20 minutes,
or until set. Top with a dollop of whipped topping and a dusting of
nutmeg before serving.

Make a sweet treat while waiting for the pie to bake. Twist
scraps of remaining pie dough and roll in a mixture of cinnamon &
sugar. Bake at 350 degrees for 10 minutes...so quick & easy!

Nana's Cheese Pie

Serves 8

1-1/2 c. graham cracker crumbs
1/3 c. plus 1/2 c. plus 3 T. sugar,
    divided
1/3 c. butter, melted

3 8-oz. pkgs. cream cheese,
    softened
2 eggs, separated and divided
1 c. sour cream

Combine cracker crumbs, 1/3 cup sugar and butter in a bowl; reserve
2 tablespoons for topping. Press crust into a 9" pie plate; set aside. In a
separate bowl, beat cream cheese, 1/2 cup sugar and egg yolks until
smooth. Beat egg whites until stiff and fold in gently. Pour into crust and
bake at 325 degrees for 20 minutes; cool. Mix sour cream and remaining
3 tablespoons sugar; spoon over cooled pie. Sprinkle with reserved
crumb mixture.

Need a special tablecloth for a dessert buffet? There are so many charming print fabrics available at craft stores. Two to three yards is all you'll need. No hemming required... just trim the edges with pinking shears!

Caramel-Banana Pie

Makes 8 servings

14-oz. can sweetened condensed
    milk
2 to 3 bananas, sliced
9-inch graham cracker pie crust

1 c. whipping cream
1/4 c. powdered sugar
2 chocolate-covered toffee candy
    bars, frozen and broken

Pour condensed milk into an 8" pie plate; cover with aluminum foil. Pour about 1/4 inch hot water into a 2-quart shallow casserole dish; place covered pie plate in casserole dish. Bake at 425 degrees for one hour and 20 minutes, or until milk is thick and caramel colored; add more water to dish if necessary. Carefully remove pan from oven; uncover and set aside. Arrange banana slices in crust; pour caramel over bananas. Cool for at least 30 minutes; while cooling, blend cream and sugar together until fluffy. Spread over caramel layer; sprinkle with toffee bar bits. Chill for 3 hours to overnight.

Chocolate shavings look so delicate but are really simple to make. Just pull a vegetable peeler across a chilled bar of chocolate and watch it curl!

Buckeye Ice Cream Pie

Makes 8 servings

1/2 c. semi-sweet chocolate chips
1/4 c. corn syrup
1/2 c. creamy peanut butter

1 qt. vanilla ice cream, softened
9-inch chocolate cookie crumb
  crust

Combine chocolate chips, corn syrup and peanut butter in a saucepan.
Cook over medium heat for 7 to 10 minutes, until melted, stirring
constantly. Remove from heat; mix in ice cream, blending until creamy.
Pour into pie crust; freeze until firm.

Toss nuts, raisins, dried or fresh fruit in flour before adding to cake or cookie batter...it keeps them from sinking to the bottom!

Chocolate Chip Cookie Pie

Serves 6 to 8

2 eggs
1/2 c. sugar
1/2 c. brown sugar, packed
3/4 c. butter, softened

1/2 c. all-purpose flour
1 c. semi-sweet chocolate chips
Optional: 1 c. chopped walnuts
9-inch pie crust

In a bowl, blend together eggs, sugars and butter; add flour, mixing well. Stir in chocolate chips and walnuts, if desired. Spread in pie crust. Bake at 325 degrees for one hour, or until center tests done.

When frosting a cake, tuck strips of wax paper under the edges of the bottom layer. Remove them after the cake is frosted for a neat and tidy cake plate with no frosting smudges.

The Queen's Strawberry Cake

Serves 8 to 10

10-oz. pkg. frozen strawberries,
   thawed
18-1/4 oz. pkg. white cake mix
1/2 c. water
1/2 c. oil
4 eggs
3-oz. pkg. strawberry gelatin mix

Drain strawberries; reserve 1/3 cup juice and set aside. Combine dry cake mix, water and oil in a bowl; beat until smooth. Add eggs, one at a time, beating after each addition. Add half of the strawberries and reserved juice. Add dry gelatin mix; blend together. Pour into a greased 13"x9" baking pan; spoon remaining strawberries on top. Bake at 350 degrees for 30 to 40 minutes. Let cool; invert onto serving plate.

A handy trick for greasing and flouring baking pans...
grease the pan, sprinkle with flour, cover with plastic wrap
and give it a good shake!

Coconut Cake

Makes 12 servings

1 lb. butter
3 c. sugar, divided
2 c. all-purpose flour, divided
6 eggs
7-oz. pkg. sweetened flaked
   coconut

1 t. vanilla extract
1/2 c. water
1 t. coconut extract
Garnish: powdered sugar

In a bowl, blend together butter and 2 cups sugar. Add one cup flour and mix well. Add eggs, one at a time, beating well after each. Add remaining flour, coconut and vanilla. Pour batter into a well greased Bundt® pan. Bake at 350 degrees for 50 minutes. Cool for 30 minutes and invert onto a serving platter. In a saucepan over medium heat, simmer together remaining sugar, water and coconut extract for 5 to 10 minutes. Baste cake with sugar mixture until all is absorbed. Before serving, dust lightly with powdered sugar. For the best flavor, cover and let stand up to 2 days before serving.

Keep apple pie spice on hand to use in all kinds of
desserts. A blend of cinnamon, nutmeg and allspice,
it's like a spice rack in a bottle!

Apple Pie Cake

Makes 8 servings

1/2 c. butter
1 egg
1 c. sugar
1 c. all-purpose flour
1 t. cinnamon
1 t. salt

1 t. baking soda
2-1/2 c. apples, peeled, cored
   and diced
2 T. boiling water
1/4 c. chopped walnuts
Garnish: whipped topping

In a bowl, blend together butter, egg and sugar. Add flour, cinnamon, salt and baking soda, mixing well. Toss together apples, water and walnuts in a separate bowl; stir into flour mixture. Pour into a greased 9" pie plate; bake at 350 degrees for 40 minutes. Serve with whipped topping.

Taking a cake to a party or potluck? Make sure the frosting will still look party-perfect when you arrive. Insert toothpicks halfway into the cake before covering in plastic wrap...they'll keep the plastic wrap from touching the frosting.

Sweet Hummingbird Cake

Serves 12

8-oz. can crushed pineapple
2 to 3 bananas, sliced
1/2 c. milk
2 eggs
1/4 c. oil

1 t. vanilla extract
Optional: 1/4 c. dark rum
18-1/2 oz. pkg. banana cake mix
16-oz. can vanilla frosting

In a bowl, beat together pineapple with juice, bananas, milk, eggs, oil, vanilla extract and rum, if using, until well blended. Stir in dry cake mix until moistened. Pour into a greased and floured Bundt® pan. Bake at 350 degrees on middle rack of oven for 40 minutes, or until cake springs back when touched. Cool for at least 45 minutes; invert onto a serving plate. Microwave frosting on high setting 15 to 20 seconds, until thin. Let stand for a minute before drizzling over cake.

Cream cheese icing is a scrumptious addition to any cake.
Blend together 1/2 cup softened cream cheese and
1/4 cup softened butter until creamy. Gradually stir in 1-1/4 cups
powdered sugar to desired consistency. Add one teaspoon
vanilla extract and use immediately.

Amish Brown Sugar Cake

Serves 12 to 15

16-oz. pkg. brown sugar
3 c. all-purpose flour
2 T. baking soda
1/2 c. butter, softened

2 c. buttermilk
1 egg, beaten
1 t. vanilla extract
1/4 c. chopped pecans

In a bowl, mix together brown sugar, flour and baking soda. In a separate bowl, blend together remaining ingredients; add to dry ingredients. Mix well. Pour into a ungreased 13"x9" baking pan. Bake at 350 degrees for 35 to 45 minutes, until a toothpick inserted in center comes out clean.

Edible flowers make a beautiful decoration for any dessert...violets, rose petals, forget-me-nots, pansies and Johnny-jump-ups. Be sure to use only pesticide-free flowers and rinse them well before using.

Lemon Cream Puff Cake

Makes 10 to 12 servings

1/2 c. butter
1 c. water
1 c. all-purpose flour
4 eggs

16-oz. container frozen whipped
   topping
Garnish: 1.55-oz. chocolate bar,
   grated into curls

Melt butter with water in a saucepan over medium heat. Remove from heat; stir in flour until dough forms into a ball. Add eggs, one at a time, mixing after each one until smooth. Spread dough to fill a lightly greased rimmed baking sheet. Bake at 400 degrees for 30 to 35 minutes, until golden; let cool. Spread Lemon Filling over crust; top with whipped topping. Garnish with chocolate curls.

Lemon Filling:

8-oz. pkg. cream cheese, softened
3 c. milk

2 5-oz. pkgs. instant lemon
   pudding mix

Blend ingredients together until thick.

Make treats ahead of time and keep them frozen to serve later. Wrap in layers of plastic wrap and aluminum foil. Freeze cookies up to 6 months, pies up to 4 months and cakes up to 2 months. Thaw in the fridge, then frost or decorate just before serving.

Cocoa & Coffee Sheet Cake

Makes 24 servings

2 c. all-purpose flour
2 c. sugar
1/2 c. shortening
1/4 c. baking cocoa
1 c. hot brewed coffee
1/2 c. butter

1 t. baking soda
1 t. vanilla extract
1/2 c. buttermilk
1 t. cinnamon
2 eggs, beaten

In a large bowl, combine flour and sugar; set aside. In a saucepan, combine shortening, cocoa, coffee and butter; bring to a boil. Slowly stir into flour mixture. Stir in remaining ingredients, mixing until well blended. Pour batter into a greased and floured 13"x9" baking pan. Bake at 400 degrees for 25 minutes. Pour frosting over cake immediately after removing cake from oven.

Frosting:

1/4 c. baking cocoa
6 T. milk
1/2 c. butter

16-oz. pkg. powdered sugar
1 t. vanilla extract
1/2 c. chopped pecans

In a saucepan, combine cocoa, milk and butter; bring to a boil. Add powdered sugar, vanilla and pecans, stirring well.

Happiness being a dessert so sweet,
May life give you more than you can ever eat.

—Irish Toast

Brownie Cupcakes

Makes 2-1/2 dozen

4 1-oz. sqs. semi-sweet baking
   chocolate
1 c. butter
1-1/2 c. chopped walnuts

1-3/4 c. sugar
1 c. all-purpose flour
4 eggs
1 t. vanilla extract

In a saucepan over low heat, melt chocolate and butter; stir in nuts and set aside. Combine sugar, flour, eggs and vanilla in a bowl; mix until well blended. Add to chocolate mixture; mix until just blended. Spoon into paper-lined muffin cups. Bake at 325 degrees for 20 to 25 minutes.

Coffee adds a rich taste to chocolate recipes...
just substitute an equal amount for water or milk in
cake, cookie or brownie recipes.

Chocolate Cabin Cake

Makes 10 to 12 servings

2 c. all-purpose flour
2 t. salt, divided
1 t. baking powder
1 t. baking soda
3/4 c. baking cocoa
2 c. sugar
1 c. oil

1 c. hot brewed coffee
1-1/4 c. milk, divided
2 eggs
2 t. vanilla extract, divided
16-oz. pkg. powdered sugar
3/4 c. butter-flavored shortening
1 t. almond extract

In a bowl, sift together flour, one teaspoon salt, baking powder, baking soda, cocoa and sugar. Add oil, coffee and one cup milk. Beat with an electric mixer on medium speed for 2 minutes. Add eggs and one teaspoon vanilla; beat for 2 minutes more. Pour into 2 greased and floured 9" cake pans. Bake at 325 degrees for 25 to 30 minutes. Cool at least 15 minutes before removing from pans. In a large bowl, beat together powdered sugar, shortening, almond extract, remaining salt, milk and vanilla for 5 minutes; ice cake.

Take-out boxes are available in plenty of festive colors and patterns. Keep some handy for wrapping up food gifts in a jiffy...and for sending home dessert with party or dinner guests who just can't eat another bite!

Harvest Apple Cheesecake

Serves 10

2 c. graham cracker crumbs
1/3 c. brown sugar, packed
1/2 c. butter, melted and divided
1 T. cinnamon
3 apples, peeled, cored and sliced
    into 12 rings
4 eggs

3/4 c. sugar
8-oz. container ricotta cheese
8-oz. pkg. cream cheese, softened
2 t. vanilla extract
8-oz. container whipping cream
Garnish: cinnamon

Combine cracker crumbs, brown sugar, 4 tablespoons butter and cinnamon in a bowl. Press on bottom and part way up sides of an ungreased 9" springform pan. In a skillet, sauté apple rings on both sides in remaining butter. Arrange apple rings on prepared crust. In a separate bowl, beat eggs, sugar, ricotta, cheeses and vanilla until smooth. Blend in cream. Pour cheese mixture into pan over apple rings. Arrange remaining apple rings on top, press apples slightly into the mixture. Sprinkle top generously with cinnamon. Bake at 450 degrees for 10 minutes, then reduce heat to 300 degrees and bake for 50 to 55 minutes. Cool and refrigerate overnight before serving.

Sparkly sugared fruit garnishes are simple to make and so pretty. Simply brush strawberries or grapes with light corn syrup, then roll in super-fine sugar.

No-Bake Cheesecake

Makes 12 to 15 servings

2-1/2 c. graham cracker crumbs
1 c. butter, melted
2 8-oz. pkgs. cream cheese,
   softened
2 c. sour cream
4 t. vanilla extract

2/3 c. sugar
16-oz. container frozen whipped
   topping, thawed
Garnish: 21-oz. can cherry
   pie filling

Toss graham cracker crumbs and butter together in a bowl; press evenly into an ungreased 13"x9" baking pan. In a bowl, stir cream cheese until smooth; add sour cream, vanilla and sugar. Fold in whipped topping; spread evenly into crust. Refrigerate overnight. Garnish with pie filling before serving.

A super-simple, easy dessert...make or buy a dreamy
white angel food cake. Make it extra luscious with strawberry
whipped cream filling, or drizzle with fresh raspberry sauce.
Garnish with sanding sugar for added sparkle.

Sweet Potato Pound Cake

Serves 10 to 12

3 c. all-purpose flour
2 t. baking powder
1 t. baking soda
1 t. salt
1-1/2 t. cinnamon
1/4 t. nutmeg
1/4 t. mace

1 c. butter, softened
1-1/2 c. sugar
1/4 c. brown sugar, packed
2-1/2 c. sweet potatoes, peeled,
　　cooked and mashed
4 eggs
1 T. vanilla extract

Whisk together flour, baking powder, baking soda, salt and spices in a
bowl. Set aside. Combine butter and sugars in a large bowl; using an
electric mixer, beat on high speed until fluffy. Beat in sweet potatoes; add
eggs, one at a time. Add flour mixture one-third at a time on low speed;
beat in vanilla. Spoon into a Bundt® pan sprayed with non-stick
vegetable spray. Bake at 350 degrees for one hour, or until cake tests
done with a toothpick. Cool cake in pan on a wire rack for 30 minutes.
Turn cake out of pan onto a cake plate.

Lighten up baked goods with ease! Applesauce can be used as a fat-free substitute for oil when baking cakes, muffins and other moist, cake-like goodies. Just substitute for some or all of the oil in the recipe.

Harvard Beet Spice Cake

Makes 8 to 10 servings

16-oz. jar Harvard beets
1/2 c. butter, softened
1-1/4 c. sugar
2 eggs, beaten
2-1/4 c. all-purpose flour
4 t. baking soda

1-1/2 t. allspice
1 t. cinnamon
1/4 t. ground cloves
1 c. chopped walnuts
Garnish: powdered sugar

Process beets in a blender until smooth; set aside. In a large bowl, beat butter with sugar until light and fluffy. Add eggs; beat well and set aside. Sift together flour, baking soda and spices. Add flour mixture to butter mixture alternately with puréed beets, mixing well after each addition. Fold in walnuts. Turn batter into a greased and lightly floured Bundt® pan. Bake at 350 degrees for 55 minutes, or until cake tests done. Cool cake in pan on a wire rack for 30 minutes. Turn cake out of pan onto a cake plate. Sift powdered sugar over cake.

Set up a coffee station for friends to enjoy while nibbling on dessert. Make it extra special by offering flavored creamers, rock candy stirring sticks and scrumptious toppings like whipped cream, cinnamon and chocolate shavings.

Grandma Rene's Crumb Cake *Makes 10 to 12 servings*

2 c. brown sugar, packed
2 c. all-purpose flour
1 c. butter, softened
1 t. baking soda
1 t. salt
1 c. milk
1 t. vanilla extract

1 t. cinnamon
1/2 t. ground cloves
1/2 t. nutmeg
1 banana, mashed
1/2 c. chopped walnuts
1/2 c. raisins
Optional: whipped cream

Combine brown sugar and flour in a large bowl; set aside 1/2 cup of mixture for crumb topping. Blend butter into remaining flour mixture. In a cup, stir baking soda and salt into milk. Add milk, vanilla, spices, banana, nuts and raisins to flour mixture. Mix well until batter is slightly lumpy. Pour batter into a greased 13"x9" baking pan. Sprinkle with reserved crumb topping; do not stir. Bake at 350 degrees for 45 minutes, or until dark golden. Top with whipped cream, if desired.

Jams and preserves keep well, so pick up a few jars of local specialties like beach plum, peach or boysenberry on family vacations. Later, use them to bake up jam cakes or thumbprint cookies...the flavors will bring back happy memories!

Jam-Swirled Coffee Cake

Makes 9 to 12 servings

2 c. all-purpose flour
1/2 c. sugar
1 T. baking powder
1/2 t. salt
1/3 c. butter

1 egg, beaten
3/4 c. milk
1/2 c. apricot preserves
1/2 c. strawberry preserves

Combine flour, sugar, baking powder and salt in a bowl; mix well. Cut in butter with a fork or pastry blender until crumbly. Add egg and milk; stir just until moistened. Spread in a greased 9"x9" baking pan. Spoon preserves over top; use a knife to swirl preserves through batter. Sprinkle evenly with topping. Bake at 400 degrees for 25 to 35 minutes. Use toothpick to check for doneness. Serve warm.

Topping:

2/3 c. brown sugar, packed
2 T. all-purpose flour

2 T. butter
1/2 c. chopped walnuts

In a small bowl, mix ingredients with a fork until crumbly.

Cake pops...kids of all ages love 'em! Make some in a jiffy
with this quick tip. Insert treat sticks in unglazed cake-type
doughnut holes and dip in melted white or semi-sweet chocolate
coating. Add candy sprinkles and stand them in a tall vase
for easy serving...done!

Glazed Honey-Walnut Bars

Makes 10 servings

1/2 c. oil
2 T. honey
1/2 c. sugar
1 egg, beaten

1 t. cinnamon
1 c. self-rising flour
1/2 c. chopped walnuts

In a bowl, mix together oil, honey, sugar and egg; set aside. In a separate bowl, stir cinnamon into flour; add to oil mixture and mix well. Stir in nuts. Spread in a greased 8"x8" baking pan. Bake at 350 degrees for 15 to 25 minutes, until set. Remove from oven; pour Glaze over top and spread. Cool; cut into bars.

Glaze:

1 c. powdered sugar
1 T. mayonnaise

1 T. milk
1 t. vanilla extract

Blend together all ingredients; mix well.

Create a charming cake stand with thrift-store finds.
Attach a glass plate with epoxy glue to a short glass vase,
tea cup or candle stand for a base. Let dry completely
before using...so clever!

Streusel-Topped Raspberry Bars

Makes 2 dozen

2-1/4 c. all-purpose flour
1 c. sugar
1 c. chopped pecans

1 c. butter, softened
1 egg
3/4 c. raspberry preserves

Combine all ingredients except preserves in a large bowl. Beat with an electric mixer on low speed until mixture resembles coarse crumbs, about 2 to 3 minutes. Set aside 2 cups of crumb mixture. Place remaining crumb mixture in a greased 9"x9" baking pan; press to cover the bottom. Spread raspberry preserves to within 1/2 inch from edges; sprinkle reserved crumb mixture over the top. Bake at 350 degrees for 40 to 50 minutes; cool completely. Cut into bars to serve.

A simply sweet idea...make a certificate for a
Dessert-of-the-Month Club! Friends will love it when
you deliver a homemade treat each month.

Buttery Lemon Snow Bars

Makes 1-1/2 dozen

2 c. sugar, divided
2-2/3 c. plus 1/4 c. all-purpose
    flour, divided
1 c. butter, softened

4 eggs, beaten
6 T. lemon juice
Garnish: powdered sugar

In a bowl, stir together 1/2 cup sugar and 2-2/3 cups flour. Cut in butter; mix until crumbly. Pat into the bottom of a greased 13"x9" baking pan. Bake at 350 degrees for 15 to 20 minutes; remove from oven. In a separate bowl, mix together eggs, lemon juice and remaining sugar and flour, blending well. Pour over baked crust and return to oven for an additional 20 minutes; cool. While still slightly warm, dust with powdered sugar.

Keep a collection of colored sugars, candy sprinkles and
edible glitter on hand to make your home-baked goodies special!
Sprinkle them on cupcakes and cookies...they'll be the hit
of the next bake sale!

Key Lime-White Chocolate Chippers

Makes 2-1/2 dozen

1/2 c. butter, softened
1 c. sugar
1 egg, beaten
1 egg yolk, beaten
1-1/2 c. all-purpose flour

1 t. baking powder
1/2 t. salt
1/4 c. lime juice
1-1/2 t. lime zest
3/4 c. white chocolate chips

Blend butter, sugar, egg and egg yolk in a large bowl; blend in flour, baking powder, salt, lime juice and lime zest. Fold in chocolate chips; roll dough into walnut-size balls. Place on ungreased baking sheets. Bake at 350 degrees for 8 to 10 minutes. Cool on a wire rack.

For orange or lemon zest in a jiffy, use a vegetable peeler
to remove very thin slices of peel. Mince finely with a
paring knife. A grater works well too.

Orange Cookies

Makes about 4 dozen

2 c. sugar
1 c. shortening
2 eggs, beaten
1 c. sour cream
juice and zest of 2 oranges,
    divided

1 T. baking soda
5 c. all-purpose flour
2 T. baking powder
1/8 t. salt
16-oz. pkg. powdered sugar
2 T. butter, melted

In a bowl, mix sugar, shortening, eggs, sour cream and juice and zest of one orange. Sift together baking soda, flour, baking powder and salt; add to egg mixture. Drop by tablespoonfuls on ungreased baking sheets. Bake at 350 degrees for 7 to 8 minutes. To make frosting, mix together remaining zest and juice, powdered sugar and butter. Frost cookies when cool.

Sprinkle powdered sugar on the work surface when
rolling out cookie dough...so much tastier than using flour
and it works just as well!

Good Neighbor Sugar Cookies   *Makes about 4 dozen*

3 c. all-purpose flour
1 t. cream of tartar
1 t. baking soda
1 t. salt

1 c. shortening
2 eggs, beaten
1 c. sugar
1 t. vanilla extract

Mix together flour, cream of tartar, baking soda and salt in a bowl. In a separate bowl, whisk together remaining ingredients with a fork. Stir shortening mixture into flour mixture. Wrap dough in plastic wrap; refrigerate for 30 minutes. On a floured surface, roll out dough 1/8-inch thick; cut into shapes with cookie cutters, as desired. Arrange on lightly greased baking sheets. Bake at 375 degrees for 5 to 6 minutes, until lightly golden.

Try using a plastic knife to cut your next pan of brownies or bar cookies...smooth edges all over!

Pecan Pie Bars

Makes 1-1/2 to 2 dozen

1-1/4 c. all-purpose flour
1/2 c. plus 3 T. brown sugar,
   packed
1/2 c. plus 2 T. margarine,
   divided

2 eggs, beaten
1/2 c. corn syrup
1 t. vanilla extract
1/2 c. chopped pecans

In a bowl, combine flour and 3 tablespoons brown sugar; cut in 1/2 cup margarine until coarse crumbs form. Press into an ungreased 11"x7" pan. Bake at 375 degrees for 20 minutes. While crust is baking, melt remaining margarine. Combine eggs, remaining brown sugar, melted margarine, corn syrup and vanilla. Blend in pecans and pour mixture onto crust. Bake for 15 to 20 minutes. Cool and cut into bars.

Such a fun treat! Fill flat-bottomed ice cream cones half full of cake batter, place on a baking sheet and bake at 350 degrees for 20 minutes. When cooled, top with scoops of ice cream.

Buttery Maple-Walnut Drops

Makes 4 dozen

2-1/4 c. all-purpose flour
1 t. baking soda
1 t. salt
1 c. butter, softened
3/4 c. sugar

3/4 c. brown sugar, packed
1-1/2 t. maple flavoring
2 eggs
1-1/2 c. chopped walnuts

Whisk together flour, baking soda and salt in a small bowl; set aside. In another bowl, beat butter, sugars and maple flavoring until creamy; beat in eggs. Gradually add flour mixture and stir in walnuts. Drop by rounded tablespoonfuls onto ungreased baking sheets, placing about 1-1/2 inches apart. Bake at 375 degrees for 9 to 11 minutes, until golden.

Plump up raisins for extra moist, tender cookies! Cover them with boiling water and let stand about 15 minutes, then drain well and pat dry. Works great with dried cranberries too.

Pumpkin-Raisin Snack Cake

Makes 2 to 3 dozen

15-oz. can pumpkin
1 c. sugar
1 c. brown sugar, packed
1/2 c. butter, melted
4 eggs
2 t. vanilla extract
1-1/2 c. all-purpose flour

2-1/2 t. pumpkin pie spice
1 t. baking powder
1/2 t. baking soda
1/4 t. salt
1 c. raisins
1/2 c. chopped walnuts
16-oz. can cream cheese frosting

Blend pumpkin, sugars, butter, eggs and vanilla in a large bowl with an electric mixer on medium speed. Combine dry ingredients in a small bowl; stir into pumpkin mixture. Add raisins and nuts. Pour into a greased 13"x9" baking pan. Bake at 350 degrees for 35 to 40 minutes, until a toothpick tests clean. Cool. Spread with frosting; let stand until set. Cut into squares.

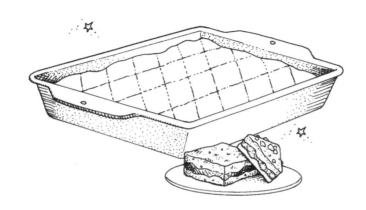

Give bar cookies a fresh new look! Instead of bars
or squares, cut cookies into diamond shapes.

Abracadabra Bars

Makes 2-1/2 dozen

1/2 c. butter, melted
1 c. graham cracker crumbs
1 c. milk chocolate chips
1 c. butterscotch chips

1 c. sweetened flaked coconut
1 c. chopped walnuts
14-oz. can sweetened condensed
   milk

Coat the bottom of 13"x9" baking pan with butter. Sprinkle with
remaining ingredients except condensed milk. Gently pour condensed
milk over top; bake at 325 degrees for 25 minutes. Cool; cut into bars.
Refrigerate until firm.

Dress up simple cookies with a yummy glaze. Combine 1/2 cup white or semi-sweet chocolate chips with one teaspoon shortening in a microwave-safe bowl. Microwave on high for one minute, stir, then drizzle over cookies.

Mom's Yummy Cookies

Makes 3 to 4 dozen

1 c. sugar
1/2 c. brown sugar, packed
1/2 c. butter, softened
2 eggs, beaten
1 t. vanilla extract
1/2 t. salt

3/4 t. baking soda
1/4 t. baking powder
2 c. corn flake cereal
1-3/4 c. all-purpose flour
2 c. semi-sweet chocolate chips
1 c. sweetened flaked coconut

In a large bowl, combine sugars, butter, eggs, vanilla, salt, baking soda and baking powder; mix well. Stir in remaining ingredients. Shape into 1-1/2 inch balls; place on greased baking sheets. Bake at 375 degrees for 7 to 8 minutes. Let cookies cool slightly before removing to a wire rack.

Watch at yard sales for interesting old single plates.
You can often find a real treasure for pennies to fill
full of yummies at the next bake sale!

Peanut Butter Temptations

Makes about 4 dozen

1/2 c. butter, softened
1/2 c. crunchy peanut butter
1/2 c. sugar
1/2 c. brown sugar, packed
1 egg, beaten
1 t. vanilla extract

3/4 t. baking soda
1/2 t. salt
1-1/4 c. all-purpose flour
48 mini peanut butter cups,
    unwrapped

Blend butter and peanut butter in a bowl; blend in sugars, egg and vanilla until light and fluffy. Add baking soda and salt; gradually mix in flour until thoroughly blended. Shape into one-inch balls; place in greased mini muffin tins. Bake at 350 degrees for 12 minutes; remove from oven. Immediately press a mini peanut butter cup into the center of each crust; cool completely before removing from pan.

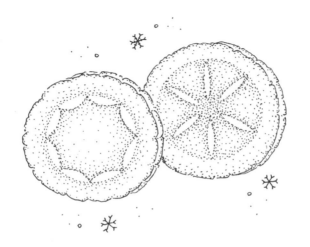

Perfect for peanut butter cookies! Check your cupboard for glass tumblers with pretty patterns on the bottom. Just dip the glass in sugar and press to flatten walnut-size balls of dough.

Flourless Peanut Butter Kisses   *Makes about 2 dozen*

1 c. creamy peanut butter
1 c. sugar
1 egg, beaten

24 milk chocolate drops,
unwrapped

Combine peanut butter, sugar and egg in a bowl; mix well. Roll into small balls and arrange on an ungreased baking sheet. Bake at 350 degrees for 12 minutes. Remove from oven; immediately press a chocolate drop in the center of each cookie.

Delight the kids with super-simple ice cream sandwiches! Place a scoop of softened ice cream on the flat bottom of one side of a cookie. Top with another cookie, bottom-side down; press gently. Enjoy right away, or wrap and freeze for up to one week.

Pecan Cookie Balls

Makes 2-1/2 to 3 dozen

1 c. butter, softened
1/4 c. powdered sugar
2 c. chopped pecans

1 T. vanilla extract
2 c. all-purpose flour
1 to 2 c. powdered sugar

Blend together butter and powdered sugar; add pecans, vanilla and flour.
Wrap dough in plastic wrap; chill for about 3 hours. Form dough into
3/4-inch balls; place on ungreased baking sheets. Bake at 350 degrees
for 10 minutes. Let cool; roll in powdered sugar.

a little
something
for you!

Pick up a pack of white paper lunch sacks and wrap up a lot of
sweet gifts in a hurry. Simply fill the bags with goodies, fold over
the tops twice and add a brightly colored sticker...done!

Soft Molasses Cookies

Makes about 5 dozen

1 c. shortening
1/4 c. molasses
1 c. brown sugar, packed
1 egg, beaten
2 t. baking soda
1/2 t. ground cloves

1/2 t. ground ginger
1 t. cinnamon
1/2 t. salt
2 c. all-purpose flour
1 c. sugar

Blend together shortening, molasses, brown sugar and egg in a large bowl; set aside. Combine dry ingredients except sugar in a separate bowl; mix well. Gradually blend dry ingredients into shortening mixture; shape dough into a ball. Wrap in wax paper; refrigerate for at least 3 hours or overnight. Shape into walnut-size balls; roll in sugar. Place on ungreased baking sheets. Bake at 375 degrees for 8 to 10 minutes; do not overbake.

INDEX

INDEX

Our Story

Back in 1984, we were next-door neighbors raising our families in the little town of Delaware, Ohio. Two moms with small children, we were looking for a way to do what we loved and stay home with the kids too. We had always shared a love of home cooking and making memories with family & friends and so, after many a conversation over the backyard fence, **Gooseberry Patch** was born.

We put together our first catalog at our kitchen tables, enlisting the help of our loved ones wherever we could. From that very first mailing, we found an immediate connection with many of our customers and it wasn't long before we began receiving letters, photos and recipes from these new friends. In 1992, we put together our very first cookbook, compiled from hundreds of these recipes and, the rest, as they say, is history.

Hard to believe it's been over 25 years since those kitchen-table days! From that original little **Gooseberry Patch** family, we've grown to include an amazing group of creative folks who love cooking, decorating and creating as much as we do. Today, we're best known for our homestyle, family-friendly cookbooks, now recognized as national bestsellers.

One thing's for sure, we couldn't have done it without our friends all across the country. Each year, we're honored to turn thousands of your recipes into our collectible cookbooks. Our hope is that each book captures the stories and heart of all of you who have shared with us. Whether you've been with us since the beginning or are just discovering us, welcome to the **Gooseberry Patch** family!

Jo Ann & Vickie

Visit our website anytime
www.gooseberrypatch.com

1·800·854·6673